Is it hard or soft?

Helen Mason

Crabtree Publishing Company
www.crabtreebooks.com

Author: Helen Mason
Publishing plan research and development:
    Reagan Miller
Project development: Clarity Content Services
Project management: Joanne Chan
Project coordinator: Kathy Middleton
Editors: Rita Vanden Heuvel, Reagan Miller
Copy editor: Dimitra Chronopoulos
Proofreader: Kelly Spence, Kylie Korneluk
Design: Pixel Hive studio
Photo research: Linda Tanaka
Production coordinator and
    prepress technician: Tammy McGarr
Print coordinator: Margaret Amy Salter

Photographs:
Cover Shutterstock; p1 rmanera/Thinkstock; p4 top Otabek Niyazov/ Thinkstock, gsagi/ Thinkstock; p5 top Kordik/Shutterstock, Fotokostic/ Shutterstock; p6 David Tanaka, Sebastian Janicki/Shutterstock, Zurijeta/Shutterstock, Africa Studio/ Shutterstock; p7 left Leah-Anne Thompson/ Shutterstock, Zurijeta/Shutterstock, Africa Studio/ Shutterstock; p8 left Alan Bailey/Shutterstock, Bryan Eastham/Shutterstock; p9 top montiannoowong/ Thinkstock, steve estvanik/ Shutterstock; p10 left Poznyakov/Shutterstock, Ingram Publishing/ Thinkstock; p11 top bikeriderlondon/Shutterstock, Getty Images/ Shutterstock, Jerry Horbert/ Shutterstock, CNK02/Shutterstock; p12 top TableMountain/Shutterstock, Eldad Carin/Shutterstock, Pincarel/Shutterstock; p13 Christopher Futcher/iStock; p14 top Photodisc/Thinkstock, Dmitry Naumov/ Thinkstock; p15 top rmanera/ Thinkstock, Digital Vision/Thinkstock; p16 top Ameng Wu/Thinkstock, Lew Robertson/Thinkstock; p17 top Ron Chapple Studios/Thinkstock, Mike Kiev/ Thinkstock, right spotmatik/ Shutterstock; p18 Photodisc/Thinkstock; p19 top Helen Mason, Aaron Amat Zaragoza/Thinkstock, Chris Johnson/ Thinkstock; p20 top left Diana Taliun/ Shutterstock, Mrsiraphol/ Shutterstock, nick willshaw/ Thinkstock, top right SOMMAI/Shutterstock, Canadapanda/ Thinkstock, Africa Studio/Shutterstock; p21 left Getty Images/ Thinkstock, right top paulaphoto/ Shutterstock, SZE FEI WONG/ Thinkstock; p22 Zoonar/Thinkstock.

Library and Archives Canada Cataloguing in Publication

Mason, Helen, 1950-, author
    Is it hard or soft? / Helen Mason.

(What's the matter?)
Includes index.
Issued in print and electronic formats.
ISBN 978-0-7787-0538-3 (bound).--ISBN 978-0-7787-0542-0 (pbk.).--
ISBN 978-1-4271-9027-7 (html).--ISBN 978-1-4271-9031-4 (pdf)

    1. Hardness--Juvenile literature. 2. Matter--Properties--Juvenile
literature. I. Title. II. Series: What's the matter? (St. Catharines, Ont.)

TA418.42.M37 2014   j620.1'126   C2014-900451-6
                                               C2014-900452-4

Library of Congress Cataloging-in-Publication Data

Mason, Helen, 1950- author.
  Is it hard or soft? / Helen Mason.
       pages cm. -- (What's the matter?)
  Includes index.
  ISBN 978-0-7787-0538-3 (reinforced library binding : alk. paper) -- ISBN 978-0-7787-0542-0 (pbk. : alk. paper) -- ISBN 978-1-4271-9027-7 (electronic html) -- ISBN 978-1-4271-9031-4 (electronic pdf)
  1. Hardness--Juvenile literature. 2. Hard materials--Juvenile literature. 3. Matter--Properties--Juvenile literature. I. Title.

TA418.42.M37 2014
620.1'126--dc23
                                               2014002267

Crabtree Publishing Company

www.crabtreebooks.com   1-800-387-7650

Printed in Canada/032014/MA20140124

Published in Canada
Crabtree Publishing
616 Welland Ave.
St. Catharines, ON
L2M 5V6

Published in the United States
Crabtree Publishing
PMB 59051
350 Fifth Avenue, 59th Floor
New York, New York 10118

Published in the United Kingdom
Crabtree Publishing
Maritime House
Basin Road North, Hove
BN41 1WR

Published in Australia
Crabtree Publishing
3 Charles Street
Coburg North
VIC 3058

What is in this book?

What is matter?

How are a soft dog and a hard car the same?

They are both made of **matter**.

You are made of matter. A soccer ball is made of matter.

All matter takes up space and has **mass**.

Mass is the amount of material in an object.

Matter has **properties**.

Size is a property. A dinosaur
is very large. An ant is very small.

6

Properties describe how something looks, feels, tastes, smells, or sounds.

A drum makes a loud noise. A whisper makes little noise.

Which words describe the properties of ice?

- cold
- hot
- black
- white
- soft
- hard

How does it feel?

Texture describes how something feels when we touch it.

We can feel if something is **hard** or **soft**.

Fur is soft. Your finger can push into fur.

A wooden chair is hard.

Soft things **compress**, or become smaller under pressure. Mud is soft. Your feet sink into it.

Hard things are **firm**. They do not compress.

Cars and trucks can drive on hard roads.

Soft things

Objects are made of different kinds of materials. It is the material that makes the object hard or soft.

Pillows are made of feathers or soft foam. These materials are soft.  The pillow is soft too.

 A sponge is soft. We use a sponge during a bath.

Sheep wool is soft. We use wool to make a sweater. The sweater feels soft too.

The fluffy part of a cotton plant is soft. They make soft cotton balls.

11

Hard things

Soft materials make things soft.
Hard materials make things hard.

 Metal is a type of rock.
Rocks are hard. Things
made from metal are hard too.

A hammer is
hard. Metal
coins are hard.

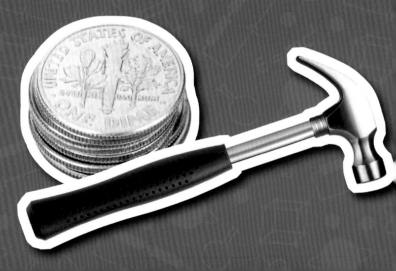

Wood comes from trees.

Wood is hard. So are wood floors.

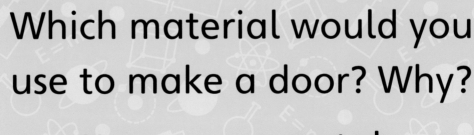

Which material would you use to make a door? Why?

- cotton
- metal
- sponge
- wood

13

Does it change shape?

Soft things change their shape.

A scarf wraps around your neck.

It keeps your neck warm.

Air fills a bouncy castle. The air makes the castle soft. It does not hurt if you fall on the castle.

Hard things do not change their shape.

A bat is hard. You can use it to hit a ball.

The top of a desk is hard. You can use it to write on.

How do hard things protect?

Hard things help in many ways.

The hard shell on
a turtle protects
its soft body.

A hard lunch box protects
your lunch. The soft food
does not get squished.

A hockey mask protects your face.

A helmet protects your head.

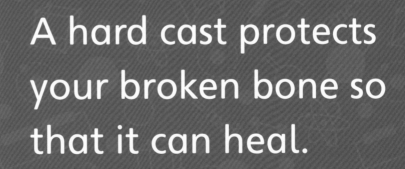

A hard cast protects your broken bone so that it can heal.

How do soft things help us?

Soft things feel good against the skin. What soft things do you like to hold?

Soft clothes feel cozy. They fit easily into a washing machine.

What soft things do you like to wear?

Babies have no teeth. They have to eat soft food.

You still like some soft foods.

Soft food is easy to swallow.

What soft foods do you like to eat? Why?

19

Be a hard and soft detective

Collect ten objects.

Which are hard?
Which are soft?

Test each to find out.

How do they feel?

Which objects change shape? Which do not?
Which words describe each object?

- feels firm
- compresses
- changes shape
- does not change shape

21

Design a chair

Design a chair. Which part should be soft? Which part should be hard?

What will you use for the hard part? Why?

- cotton
- plastic
- sponge
- wood

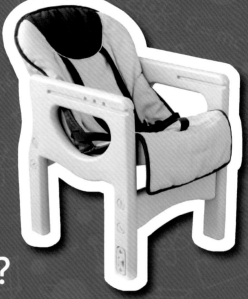

What will you use for the soft part? Why?

Words to know and Index

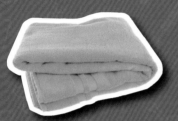

compress

pages 9, 21

firm

page 9, 21

hard

pages 4, 7–10, 12–13, 15–17, 20–22

mass

page 5

matter

pages 4–6

properties

pages 6–7

soft

pages 4, 7–12, 14, 16, 18–22

23

Notes for adults

Objectives
- to introduce the difference between hard and soft objects
- to learn how people use hard and soft objects in everyday life

Prerequisite
Ask the children to read *Is it flexible or rigid?* before reading *Is it hard or soft?*
Introducing them to the concepts of flexible and rigid will help familiarize them with
some of the ideas discussed in this book.

Questions before reading *Is it hard or soft?*
"What things are soft? What things are hard?"

"Tell me about soft things you use. What makes them soft?"

"How are hard things different from soft things?"

"How do you use hard things?"

Discussion
Read the book with the children. Discuss with the children some of the main concepts
in the book: hard and soft, firm, and compressible.

Have the children collect toys, such as a teddy bear, a model car, different balls, a
wooden block, and so on. Ask them to line up the toys according to how hard or soft
each is. Have them test each item using the test on page 21.

Extension
Collect uncooked pasta, potato chips, licorice whips, pieces of celery or carrot, slices
of fresh bread, and apple sauce. Have the children decide which items are hard and
which are soft. Ask them to choose one item. How can they harden it if it's soft or
soften it if it's hard?

Challenge the children to collect a number of hard objects. Can they scratch these
objects with a fingernail? Have them classify each according to how easy it is to
scratch.